NATURE RIDDLES

WHAT'S THAT SHADOW?

A Photo Riddle Book

By Christopher L. Harbo

CAPSTONE PRESS
a capstone imprint

A+ Books are published by Capstone Press,
151 Good Counsel Drive, P.O. Box 669, Mankato, Minnesota 56002.
www.capstonepress.com

092009
005620LKS10

 Books published by Capstone Press are manufactured with paper
containing at least 10 percent post-consumer waste.

Library of Congress Cataloging-in-Publication Data
Harbo, Christopher L.
    What's that shadow? : a photo riddle book / by Christopher L. Harbo.
    p. cm. — (A+ books. Nature riddles)
    Includes bibliographical references and index.
    Summary: "Photographs and simple text present a variety of shadows and facts
about how shadows are made" — Provided by publisher.
    ISBN 978-1-4296-3920-0 (library binding)
    1. Shades and shadows — Juvenile literature. 2. Picture puzzles — Juvenile
literature. I. Title. II. Series.
QC381.6.H37 2010
535'.4 — dc22   2009040496

Credits
Jenny Marks, editor; Veronica Bianchini, designer; Svetlana Zhurkin, media researcher;
    Laura Manthe, production specialist

Photo Credits
Alamy/WorldFoto, 21, 22
Capstone Studio/Karon Dubke, 13, 14, 27, 28, 32
Dreamstime/Denis Radovanovic, 24
Getty Images/Aurora/Carl D. Walsh, 15, 16; Check Six/George Hall, 10; Photographer's
    Choice/Kim Heacox, 25, 26; Taxi/Nick Dolding, 23
iStockphoto/Max Homand, 8
Peter Arnold/Biosphoto/Cyril Ruoso, 17, 18
Shutterstock/AZPworldwide, 19, 20; ethylalkohol, 6–7; Galina Barskaya, 29; Luo Xi, 9;
    Marcin-linfernum, 4–5; Neale Cousland, cover; Philip Lange, 11; Vladimir Wrangel, 12

Note to Parents, Teachers, and Librarians
Nature Riddles uses a nonfiction riddle format to introduce science concepts to young readers. *What's That Shadow?* is designed to be read aloud to a pre-reader, or to be read independently by an early reader. Deciphering word riddles and analyzing photos engages readers' critical thinking skills and heightens visual literacy. Nature Riddles promotes practice of the scientific inquiry process, through engaging children in observing, analyzing, guessing, and solving each science riddle.

TABLE of CONTENTS

INTRODUCTION

Don't look now, but you're being followed. A dark shape tracks your every move. When you walk, it walks. When you jump, it jumps too. What could it be? Your shadow, of course!

When the sun is out, your shadow is never far behind. A shadow is a dark shape made by something blocking light. Your body is perfect for making shadows. Light can pass by it, but it can't pass through it. Your body forms shadows where the light is blocked.

The shape of a shadow is sometimes called a silhouette.

A silhouette is the dark shape of an object seen on a lighter background. When light hits an object directly, a perfect silhouette forms.

Sometimes light hits objects at an angle. In the early morning and late afternoon, the sun is low in the sky. Shadows stretch out long. The shapes look larger than the objects making them. Guessing what made the shadows can get tricky.

CAN YOU GUESS WHAT MADE THE SHADOWS IN EACH PICTURE?

LAND SHARK

Turning green fields from light to dark,
my shadow is a huge land shark.
When it hunts you, please don't fret.
It's just a harmless silhouette.
Turn your eyes up to the sky,
and you may spy me flying high.

WHAT'S THAT SHADOW?

AN AIRPLANE!

Low-flying airplanes cast huge shadows. As planes jet across the sky, their shadows seem to swim over hills and fields.

LENGTHY LEGS

Our legs look long on a hot sand dune
as the sun goes down in the afternoon.
But if desert travel is your plan,
you may join our caravan.
Just find a seat between two humps
and watch the road for sudden bumps.

WHAT'S THAT SHADOW?

CAMELS!

A group of camels and riders is called a caravan. In afternoon sunlight, their shadows stretch out. The camels' long legs look like stilts. Their humps blend with their riders.

THE ACTOR

I'm an actor who loves nights.
I dance for you in front of lights.
I'll cast a shape that is not me.
Can you guess what I could be?
My shadow flickers on the wall,
but I can't bark or bite at all.

WHAT'S THAT SHADOW?

A SHADOW PUPPET!

Shadow puppets use light to trick your eyes. With the right pose, hands cast shadows that look like dogs, birds, or butterflies. What kinds of shadow puppets can you make?

STICK FIGURE

Take a look at my outline quick,
and you will think I'm a skinny stick.
But look again and you will see
the arms and legs attached to me.
I strike a pose. I dance a jig.
The sunlight makes my shadow big.

WHAT'S THAT SHADOW?

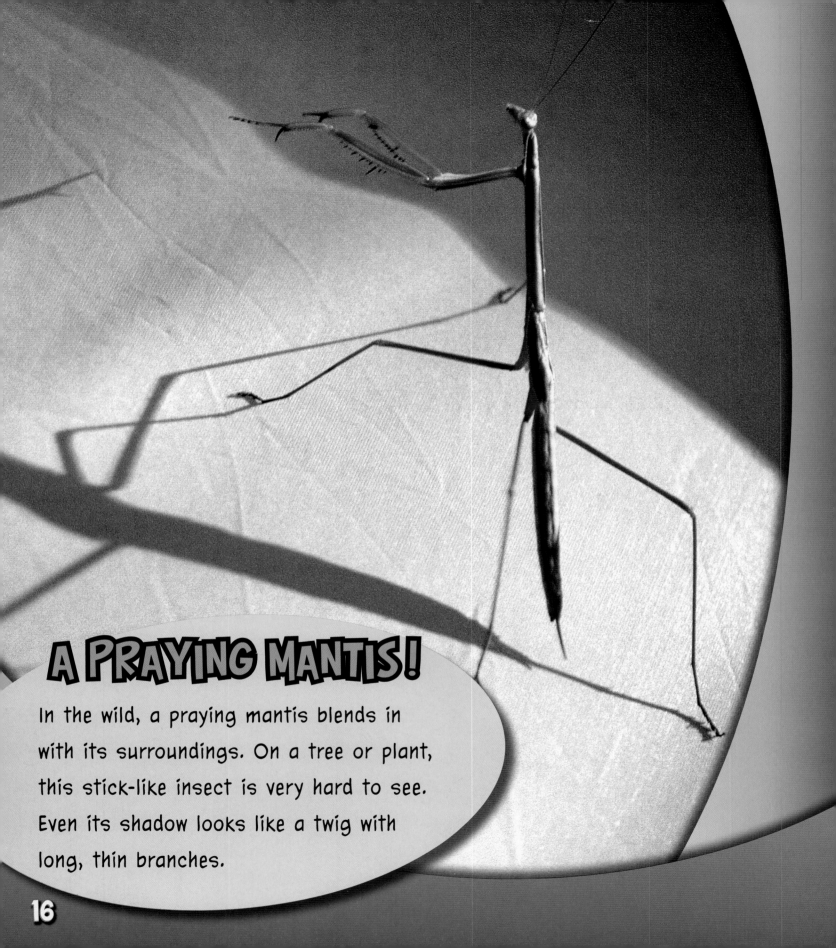

A PRAYING MANTIS!

In the wild, a praying mantis blends in with its surroundings. On a tree or plant, this stick-like insect is very hard to see. Even its shadow looks like a twig with long, thin branches.

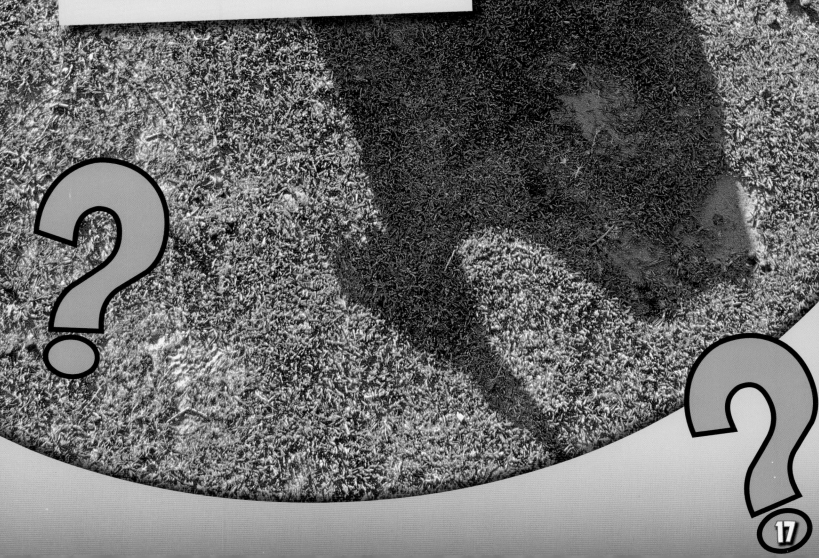

CAMEL-BUNNY

My head looks like a long-eared bunny,
but my back is shaped a little funny.
Are those camel humps you see?
A camel-bunny? How can that be?
Perhaps some hints are what you need.
I have a pouch and bounce with speed.

WHAT'S THAT SHADOW?

A KANGAROO!

Sometimes shadows make objects look strange. In the right light, one half of the kangaroo's shadow looks like a rabbit. The other half looks like a camel. That's one mixed-up shadow!

CURVES

I twist across the burning sand
without the help of feet or hands.
My shadow curves like a winding river.
But beware the bite my fangs deliver.
My tail will rattle when I'm near.
It breaks the silence loud and clear.

WHAT'S THAT SHADOW?

A Rattlesnake!

The sidewinder rattlesnake makes a smooth, curving shadow on the sand. Did you notice the little bump sticking up on its head? That shadow is made by horn-shaped scales above the snake's eyes.

MONSTER

I saw a monster on the beach,
his legs and horns within my reach.
I tried to run far, far away.
But by my side he'd always stay.
His shape grows in the afternoon.
I fear his claws will pinch me soon.

WHAT'S THAT SHADOW?

A CRAB!

You might jump if this crab's shadow snuck up on you at the beach. Its legs and claws stretch into the shape of a giant spider. The crab's eyes give the shadow a long pair of horns.

SHREDDING

Check out my shadow in the air.
Where it lands I do not care.
I can't worry where it's heading.
I just need to keep on shredding.
If I practice and don't slip,
I'll finally score a rad kickflip.

WHAT'S THAT SHADOW?

A SKATEBOARDER!

While a skateboarder flies through the air, his shadow mirrors the trick. Sunlight captures his movements in a perfect silhouette. Hope he lands safely!

24

FRIENDSHIP

Our walking waddle gently sways
to the sound of lapping waves.
Our friendship runs the ocean deep.
The promises we make, we keep.
We know we'll always be together
in tuxedos made of feathers.

WHAT'S THAT SHADOW?

PENGUINS!

Penguins make most people think of snow. But king penguins like to live on sandy island beaches near Antarctica. The shadows of these king penguins look like two friends on a sunset stroll.

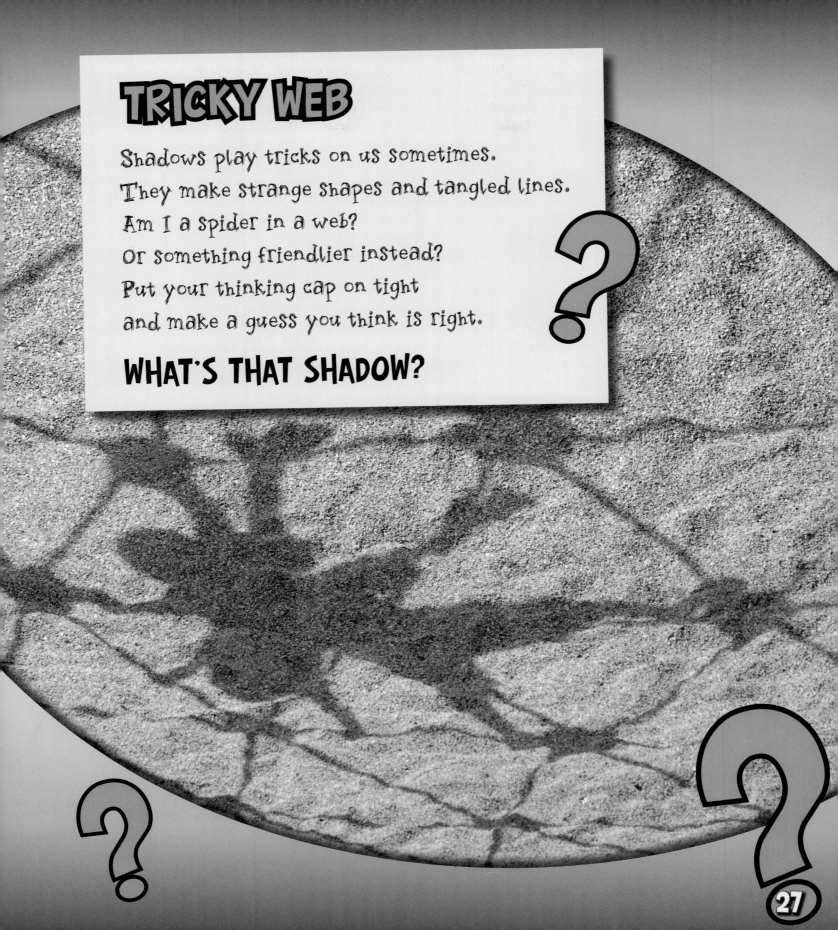

TRICKY WEB

Shadows play tricks on us sometimes.
They make strange shapes and tangled lines.
Am I a spider in a web?
Or something friendlier instead?
Put your thinking cap on tight
and make a guess you think is right.

WHAT'S THAT SHADOW?

KIDS ON A JUNGLE GYM!

Did you guess correctly? Sometimes shadows aren't what they seem. The shadow of two children playing on a jungle gym looks like a spider in a web. Now that's one tricky shadow!

28

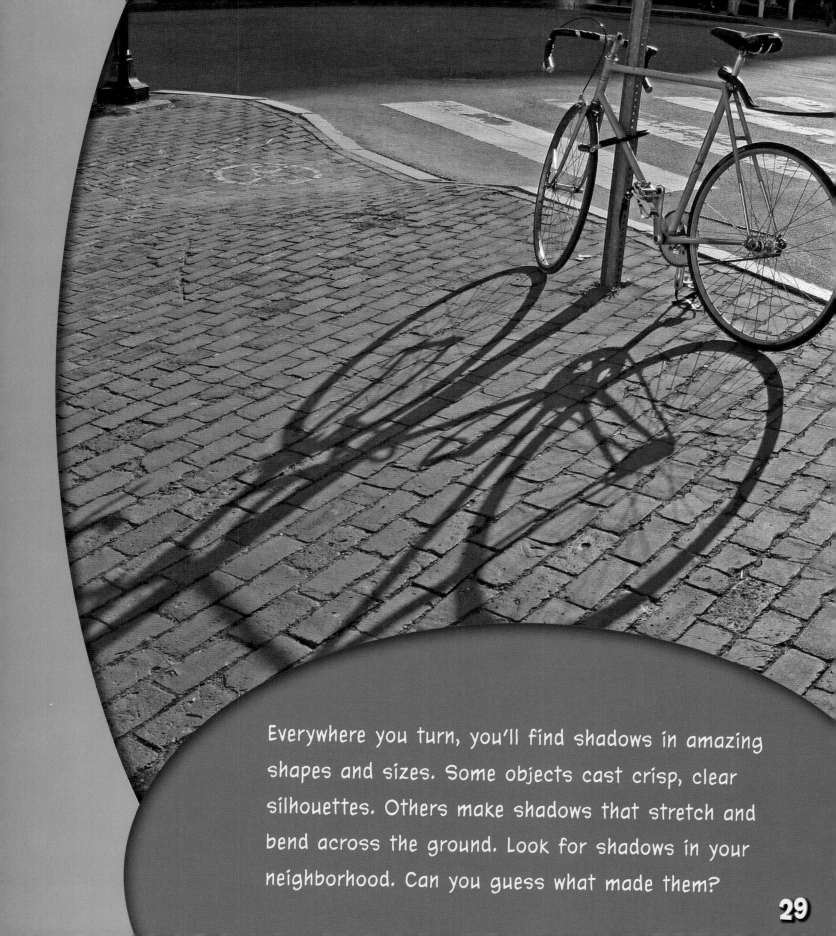

Everywhere you turn, you'll find shadows in amazing shapes and sizes. Some objects cast crisp, clear silhouettes. Others make shadows that stretch and bend across the ground. Look for shadows in your neighborhood. Can you guess what made them?

GLOSSARY

angle — sloping and not straight

caravan — people traveling together

cast — to cause or make

dune — a sand hill made by the wind

flicker — to move back and forth unsteadily

release — to free or let go of something

shred — to practice tricks on a skateboard

silhouette — the dark shape of an object
seen on a lighter background

spy — to see something

stroll — a slow, easy walk

tangle — to twist together in a messy bunch

waddle — to walk with short steps, swaying
side to side

READ MORE

Berge, Claire. *Whose Shadow Is This?: A Look at Animal Shapes — Round, Long, and Pointy.* Whose Is It? Minneapolis: Picture Window Books, 2005.

Higgins, Nadia. *Super Shadows.* Science Rocks! Edina, Minn.: Magic Wagon, 2009.

Waters, Jennifer. *Bright Lights and Shadowy Shapes.* Spyglass Books. Minneapolis: Compass Point Books, 2002.

INTERNET SITES

FactHound offers a safe, fun way to find Internet sites related to this book. All of the sites on FactHound have been researched by our staff.

Here's all you do:

Visit *www.facthound.com*

FactHound will fetch the best sites for you!

INDEX

ABOUT THE AUTHOR

In elementary school, Christopher L. Harbo read every Dr. Seuss book in the library. Stories such as *McElligot's Pool* and *If I Ran the Circus* inspired him to write his own clever rhymes. Today, Christopher still loves reading and writing. His bookshelves are loaded with rhyming books, comic books, and graphic novels. When he's not reading, Christopher also enjoys folding origami animals and watching movies.